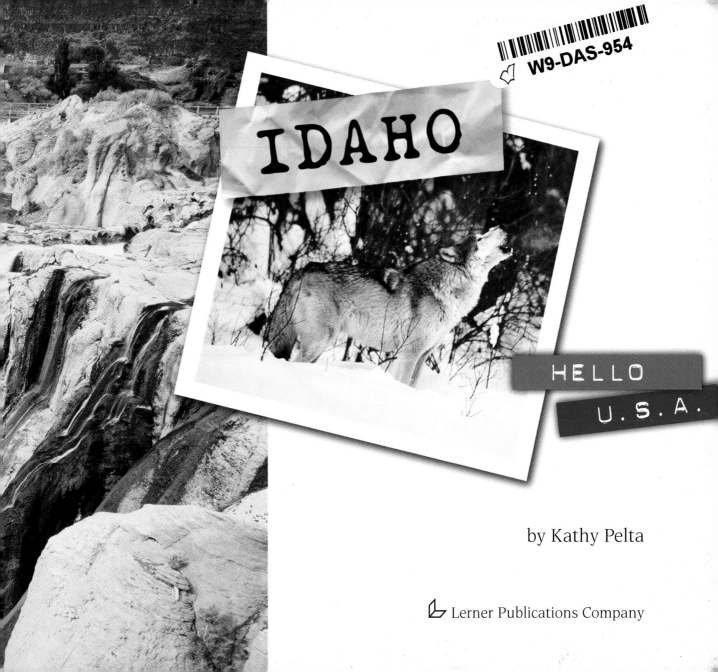

IDAHO

HELLO
U.S.A.

by Kathy Pelta

Lerner Publications Company

You'll find this picture of syringa flowers at the beginning of each chapter. The syringa flower was adopted as Idaho's official state flower in 1931 and appears on the state seal. The syringa shrub is often called mock orange because its flowers smell like orange blossoms. Long before Idaho was a state, Native Americans used the shrub's stems to make items such as pipes, cradles, and bows and arrows.

Cover (left): McGowan Peak over Stanley Lake, Sawtooth National Forest, Idaho. Cover (right): Sack of potatoes. Pages 2–3: Shoshone Falls in the Snake River near Twin Falls, Idaho. Page 3: Wolf howling in the snow.

This book is available in two editions:
Library binding by Lerner Publications Company, a division of Lerner Publishing Group
Soft cover by First Avenue Editions, an imprint of Lerner Publishing Group
241 First Avenue North
Minneapolis, MN 55401 U.S.A.

Website address: www.lernerbooks.com

Library of Congress Cataloging-in-Publication Data

Pelta, Kathy.
    Idaho / by Kathy Pelta (Rev. and expanded 2nd ed.)
       p.   cm. — (Hello U.S.A.)
    Includes index.
    Summary: Introduces the geography, history, industries, people, and other highlights of the Gem State.
    ISBN: 0–8225–4080–0 (lib. bdg. : alk. paper)
    ISBN: 0–8225–0777–3 (pbk. : alk. paper)
    1. Idaho—Juvenile literature. [1. Idaho.] I. Title. II. Series.
F746.3 .P45 2002
979.6—dc21   2001006138

Manufactured in the United States of America
1 2 3 4 5 6 – JR – 07 06 05 04 03 02

IDAHO

ALASKA

CANADA

PACIFIC
OCEAN

UNITED
STATES

HAWAII

PUERTO
RICO

MEXICO

CONTENTS

The Snake River spills over a low dam at Idaho Falls, Idaho.

THE LAND

The Gem State

 daho is a state of surprises and contrasts. It has prairies and mountains, lava flows and sand dunes, ice caves and hot springs. White-water rivers tumble through steep canyons, and thick evergreen forests surround mountain lakes. Some of the state's wilderness areas have no roads and can only be explored on foot, on horse-back, or by river raft. Several streambeds have been mined for gold and silver, as well as dozens of varieties of gemstones—which is why Idaho's nickname is the Gem State.

To the west, beyond the neighboring states of Washington and Oregon, lies the Pacific Ocean. For this reason, Idaho is called a Pacific Northwest state.

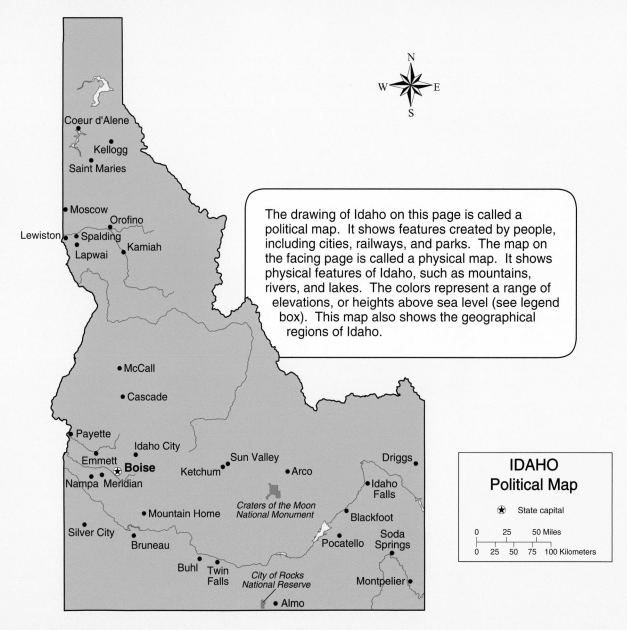

The drawing of Idaho on this page is called a political map. It shows features created by people, including cities, railways, and parks. The map on the facing page is called a physical map. It shows physical features of Idaho, such as mountains, rivers, and lakes. The colors represent a range of elevations, or heights above sea level (see legend box). This map also shows the geographical regions of Idaho.

Coeur d'Alene

Kellogg

Saint Maries

Moscow

Orofino

Lewiston • Spalding

Lapwai

Kamiah

McCall

Cascade

Payette

Idaho City

Emmett

Boise

Sun Valley

Ketchum

Driggs

Arco

Idaho Falls

Nampa Meridian

Craters of the Moon National Monument

Mountain Home

Blackfoot

Silver City

Pocatello

Soda Springs

Bruneau

Buhl

Twin Falls

City of Rocks National Reserve

Montpelier

Almo

IDAHO
Political Map

⍟   State capital

0	25	50 Miles

0	25	50	75	100 Kilometers

N
W   E
S

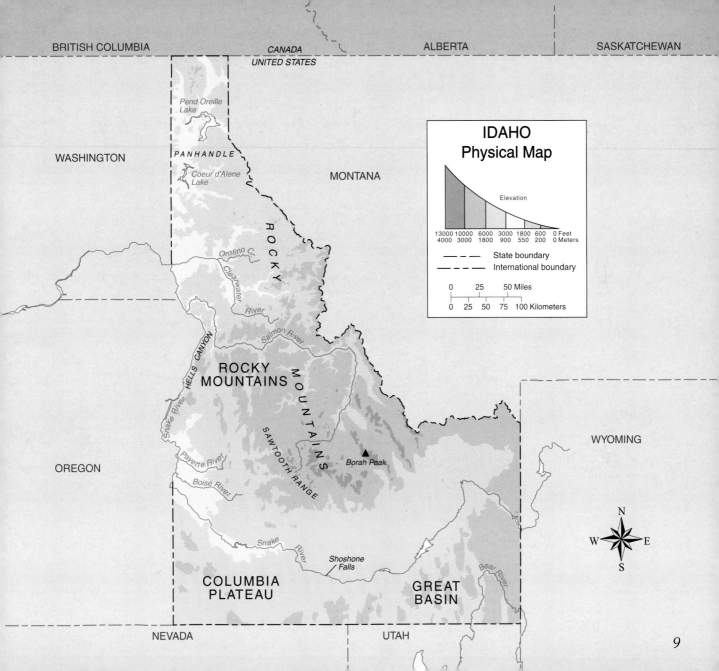

BRITISH COLUMBIA

CANADA
UNITED STATES

ALBERTA

SASKATCHEWAN

WASHINGTON

Pend Oreille Lake

PANHANDLE

Coeur d'Alene Lake

MONTANA

R O C K Y

IDAHO
Physical Map

Elevation

| 13000 | 10000 | 6000 | 3000 | 1800 | 600 | 0 Feet |
| 4000 | 3000 | 1800 | 900 | 550 | 200 | 0 Meters |

--- — State boundary
— — International boundary

| 0 | 25 | 50 Miles |
| 0 | 25 | 50 | 75 | 100 Kilometers |

Orofino Cr.

Clearwater

River

Salmon River

ROCKY
MOUNTAINS

M
O
U
N
T
A
I
N
S

HELLS CANYON

Snake River

SAWTOOTH RANGE

▲
Borah Peak

WYOMING

OREGON

Payette River

Boise River

Snake

River

Shoshone Falls

Bear River

N
W   E
S

COLUMBIA
PLATEAU

GREAT
BASIN

NEVADA

UTAH

The Sawtooth Range runs through central Idaho. The range is part of the Rocky Mountain region.

Nevada and Utah are Idaho's southern neighbors. Across the mountains to the east are Montana and Wyoming. To the north lies British Columbia, a province of Canada.

Idaho has three main land regions—the Rocky Mountains, the Columbia Plateau, and the Great Basin. The Rocky Mountain region covers three-fourths of the state, stretching from the panhandle (a narrow strip of land) in the north to southeastern Idaho. Part of a huge mountain system, the Rockies run from Canada to New Mexico.

The Rockies were formed millions of years ago, when massive rocks shoved up through the earth's crust. Thick sheets of ice called **glaciers** later carved valleys into the mountains. Borah Peak, Idaho's highest point, soars 12,662 feet above sea level. As the glaciers melted, they filled hollow areas and created numerous lakes, including Pend Oreille and Coeur d'Alene. Rivers such as the Snake, the Salmon, and the Clearwater gradually cut deep canyons in the land.

Great flows of hot volcanic lava once oozed through cracks in the earth. When it hardened into rock, the lava formed a vast **plateau,** or highland, called the Columbia Plateau. Part of this plateau extends across southern Idaho.

Shoshone Falls plunge 212 feet over a rock cliff created by the Snake River.

In some parts of Idaho's Great Basin, farmers raise wheat.

The Snake River, named for its many twists and turns, arcs across the Columbia Plateau. The waters of the Snake and its many branches have been channeled to fields of grain and vegetable crops. This system of **irrigation** has made Idaho an important food-producing state.

Hot and cold mineral springs bubble up from underneath the Columbia Plateau. The waters of Warm Springs, near the capital city of Boise, are pumped into pipes to heat some homes.

Volcanoes helped create Idaho's smallest region— the Great Basin. Part of a much larger region that stretches across Utah and Nevada, the Great Basin has flat, sandy plains and grassy plateaus. Mountain ranges in Idaho's Great Basin reach almost 10,000 feet. The Bear River, the main waterway in the region, flows southward into Great Salt Lake in Utah.

Although Idaho sits on the Canadian border, the state's high mountains block out the cold winds and blizzards that sweep southward from Canada. Warm breezes blow eastward across the state from the Pacific Ocean.

Valleys are the warmest spots in Idaho, while mountain towns are the coolest. Summer days can be hot, reaching 90°F or more in some places. But at night, the thermometer drops to around 50°F. Winter temperatures range from 10°F to 25°F or more. The mountains and valleys of the panhandle receive the most rain and snow, while the Columbia Plateau and the Great Basin remain dry throughout the year.

Idaho's rugged mountains experience some of the coldest temperatures in the state.

Idaho has a variety of plant life, including dry sagebrush.

  Forests of pine, cedar, fir, and aspen trees cover nearly 40 percent of Idaho. Deer and chipmunks dart through the woods and meadows. Wilderness areas shelter black bears, cougars, moose, and elks.

Surefooted bighorn sheep and Rocky Mountain goats climb the mountainsides. Lizards and rattlesnakes slither among the sagebrush in the state's dry regions.

Idaho's deep lakes and rushing streams hold a wide variety of fish, including salmon, trout, and sturgeon. Along a rugged canyon of the Snake River, golden eagles, hawks, and falcons nest in a national refuge for birds of prey.

In the state's cooler areas, mountain goats *(below left)* and moose *(below)* are found.

THE HISTORY

Striking It Rich

he first people to settle in what became Idaho were hunters who arrived while searching for game about 13,000 years ago. On the walls of the caves they lived in, these people painted, carved, and scratched pictures of hunters and their prey, which included mammoths and giant bison. The descendants of these hunters are called Native Americans, or American Indians.

The largest and most powerful Indian group in what became Idaho called itself Ne-Mee-Poo, meaning "the people." French fur traders who arrived much later called these Indians the Nez Perce because some had pierced noses. Like the Coeur

Over centuries, the Snake River cut the deepest gorge in North America—Hells Canyon *(left)*. Native Americans in the area knew this rugged terrain well. Ancient people carved pictures onto the sides of cliffs in southwestern Idaho *(above)*.

d'Alene, the Kalispel, the Kutenai, and other tribes in the northern and central mountains, the Nez Perce lived along river valleys. In the dry lands to the south lived the Shoshone, the Bannock, and the Paiute Indians.

Native Americans in the area that became Idaho gathered camas lily bulbs. The bulbs look like onions and taste like sweet potatoes.

All of the nations, or tribes, in the area that became Idaho traded with other groups to the east and west. They fished for salmon and hunted game, but one of their main sources of food was the bulb of the blue-flowered camas lily. Using sharp sticks, the Indians dug up the bulbs, dried them, and ground them into flour for cooking.

In the 1700s, the Nez Perce and the Shoshone began trading with other groups for horses. On horseback, the Indians crossed the Rocky Mountains to hunt bison on the Great Plains, hundreds of miles to the east. From the Plains Indians they learned to construct leather tepees and make pemmican, a food made with dried bison meat.

In the early 1800s, the U.S. government sent the explorers Meriwether Lewis and William Clark to find a route west to the Pacific Ocean. By 1805 the men had reached the Rocky Mountains in what became Idaho. They rested at a Nez Perce village for a month before continuing their journey to the Pacific Ocean.

Horses, which the Spaniards had brought earlier to North America, changed the lifestyle of many Indians, including the Nez Perce *(above)*.

When they returned home, Lewis and Clark reported that many beavers lived in what they called the Oregon Country. This region included what later became Washington, Oregon, and Idaho, as well as parts of Montana and Wyoming. Some members of the Lewis and Clark expedition stayed in the mountains to trap beavers.

Trappers known as mountain men faced harsh winters, grizzly bears, and other hazards. Many of

In 1805 Lewis and Clark became the first white people to visit the Idaho region.

Mountain men trapped
beavers in the area's forests.

them died or left the area, unable to survive
the dangers. Those who remained earned
good money for their beaver pelts, which
were used to make expensive hats for
gentlemen in Europe.

The United States and Great Britain both
claimed the region where the mountain
men worked. In 1809 David Thompson, a
Canadian explorer and mapmaker, built a
trading post on Pend Oreille Lake. Called
Kullyspell House, it was the first post in
what later became Idaho.

The next year, American trappers started a trading
post farther south, on a fork of the Snake River. At
these posts, mountain men and Indian trappers
traded beaver furs for supplies such as salt, flour,
sugar, blankets, and gunpowder.

To protect their trading posts in the Oregon Country, the United States and Great Britain each built strongholds. Nathaniel Wyeth, an American businessman from Boston, built Fort Hall on the Snake River in 1834. The Hudson's Bay Company, a British fur company, set up Fort Boise on the Boise River.

Religious teachers called **missionaries** were soon arriving to instruct the Indians about Christianity. A band of Nez Perce guided Protestant missionaries Henry and Eliza Spalding to Lapwai, along the Clearwater River. There the Spaldings built a house and a mission school.

Henry Spalding persuaded many Nez Perce to give up their traditional beliefs and customs, including their style of dress and hair. Those who would not change were whipped, which caused many Nez Perce to turn against Spalding and forced him to leave the region.

Farther north, a Catholic priest named Pierre-Jean de Smet built the Cataldo Mission in 1842 to teach the Coeur d'Alene Indians who lived in the area about the Catholic faith. Some of these Indians

Henry Spalding

helped build the mission. It still stands and is the oldest building in Idaho.

At the same time, American explorers Kit Carson and John C. Frémont were mapping a trail used by fur trappers along the Snake River. Their 1843 expedition proved that a safe journey across the dry Columbia Plateau was possible.

In 1842 Pierre-Jean de Smet chose the site where he would build the Cataldo Mission.

Wagon trains began passing through the area in the 1840s. At Three Island Crossing *(above)*, the pioneers crossed the Snake River, where the water was shallow.

Soon settlers were driving covered wagons along this path, which became known as the Oregon Trail. Moving at the rate of about 12 miles a day, they stopped at Fort Hall and Fort Boise to rest, repair their wagons, and buy supplies. At Soda Springs, the thirsty travelers drank water that bubbled up from the ground.

In 1846 the United States and Great Britain signed a **treaty,** or agreement, to split the Oregon Country between them. The United States took control of land south of what later became the border between the United States and Canada. Two years later, the United States named its possession the Oregon Territory.

U.S. officials met with Nez Perce leaders in 1855 to convince them to give up much of their homeland. The officials encouraged the Nez Perce to settle on a **reservation** in the central part of what later became Idaho. The Native Americans knew that if they didn't sign the treaty, the U.S. government would probably force them to give up their homeland, so they agreed to the deal. The Nez Perce were paid less than eight cents an acre for their land, but they were told that non-Indians would not be permitted on the reservation.

This promise, however, was soon broken. In 1860 a prospector discovered gold on reservation land at Orofino Creek. Shortly afterward, fortune hunters began arriving from all over the world.

The newcomers took steamships up the Columbia and Snake Rivers as far as the Clearwater River. The miners then walked or rode horses into the hills and raised tents on Nez Perce land. The town of Lewiston became a bustling supply center for the gold seekers. Sawmills cut lumber for buildings and for mining operations. Stables and stores sold horses and everyday goods.

The prospectors asked the U.S. government to move the boundaries of the Nez Perce reservation so the gold wouldn't be on the Indians' land. None of the Nez Perce leaders thought the request was fair— it broke the treaty they had recently signed. But they couldn't stop miners from trespassing, and some of the leaders eventually signed another treaty that made the reservation smaller.

With gold discoveries bringing in more and more people, the U.S. government voted to make this new area of wealth a separate territory. On March 4, 1863, President Abraham Lincoln signed a bill creating the Idaho Territory.

Chief Joseph, a Nez Perce leader, wanted to stay on his homeland in Oregon's Wallowa Valley instead of moving to a reservation in central Idaho. The U.S. Army chased him and his people through the mountains of Idaho and Montana before cold and hunger forced him to surrender. In a famous speech he said, "I will fight no more forever."

Chief Joseph

Meanwhile, non-Indians had begun to settle on the homelands of the Bannock and the Shoshone. The newcomers planted crops, raised livestock, and dug the first irrigation ditches in the region. They also shot the buffalo these Indians depended on for food and clothing. To defend their hunting grounds, the Indians burned grass to starve the settlers' live-stock. They also attacked farmers and wagon trains.

What's in a Name?

Many stories have been told about how Idaho got its name. But most historians believe that Idaho doesn't mean anything in any language. The name first appeared in 1860, when the steamboat *Idaho* began carrying gold seekers up the Columbia River to Lewiston. The owner of the steamboat had gotten the name from a Colorado miner, who said it was an Indian word meaning "gem of the mountains."

People started calling the gold mines near Lewiston the Idaho mines, and the name Idaho was chosen for the territory and eventually for the state. Not until the 1950s did people learn that the miner's story about the Indian meaning was a fake.

To stop these attacks, the U.S. government sent in troops. In the Massacre at Boa Ogoi in 1863, soldiers surrounded a Shoshone camp and killed more than 300 Indians. A few years later, the Shoshone signed a treaty and agreed to move to the Fort Hall reservation.

The Bannock also agreed to settle on the Fort Hall reservation as long as they could still gather camas bulbs each summer. When settlers let their hogs root out the bulbs, fighting erupted. U.S. troops defeated the Indians in what became known as the Bannock War of 1878.

After the conflict ended, settlers claimed most of Idaho's rich farmland. During the 1870s, railroad tracks were laid across the territory, and freight trains began carrying crops and livestock to markets in the Midwest. Passenger trains brought in more settlers.

By this time, most of Idaho's gold had been mined. But a new rush began when silver was discovered in 1884. Large companies bought land and hired workers to mine the silver, lead, and zinc found in the hills around Coeur d'Alene, in Idaho's panhandle.

Reservation Life

Shoshone and Bannock Indians agreed to settle on the Fort Hall reservation *(above)*, which was too small to allow them to continue to hunt and gather food. Instead they learned to farm and depended on meager food supplies from the U.S. government. In 1880 a group of Shoshone *(above inset)* from Idaho's Lemhi reservation traveled to Washington, D.C. There, they signed a treaty that eventually allowed them to move to the more fertile land of the Fort Hall reservation.

Many people were miners *(left)* when Idaho became a state in 1890. Others made use of the farmland, including this vegetable merchant in Idaho City *(below)*.

    With miners and farmers moving to Idaho, the population of the territory grew rapidly. In 1889 residents wrote a **constitution** (set of laws), and on July 3, 1890, Idaho became the 43rd state. An additional group of newcomers—Chinese and other Asians—arrived at about the time of statehood.

Farmers and miners prospered in the new state, but trouble soon developed in the Idaho panhandle. To fight for better wages and working conditions, many of the miners had joined **labor unions** (workers' organizations).

After the price of silver fell in 1892, mine owners tried to cut the wages they paid their workers. When union miners protested, mine owners replaced them with nonunion employees. This led to fighting between union and nonunion miners.

During another union protest in 1899, hundreds of miners set off an explosion at the Bunker Hill mine. Governor Frank Steunenberg called in U.S. troops, who arrested the miners. For the next two years, miners could not work without a permit saying they had not helped dynamite the Bunker Hill.

Despite the unrest, Idaho's economy continued to grow in the early 1900s. Logging companies began to buy huge forests in northern and central Idaho. Shipping the lumber to eastern markets was expensive, but eventually logging would earn the state more money than mining.

Union Leaders Victorious

In 1899 Governor Frank Steunenberg sent U.S. troops to arrest miners who had bombed Idaho's Bunker Hill mine after the owners refused to improve working conditions. Six years later, on a December evening in 1905, the former governor opened his backyard gate, and a homemade bomb exploded and killed him. The murder led to the most famous trial in Idaho's history.

The trial pitted rich mine owners against members of the Western Federation of Miners union, who were accused of hiring a man to kill Steunenberg. Newspapers nationwide followed the case, as Americans watched the headlines.

Clarence Darrow

William E. Borah, a lawyer and U.S. senator from Idaho, led the prosecution, bringing charges against the union leaders. A famous Chicago lawyer named Clarence Darrow defended the union leaders.

As the case unfolded, Darrow skillfully shifted attention away from the specific actions of the union leaders. He focused instead on the good that unions in general were trying to achieve for working-class Americans.

After weighing the evidence for nine hours, a jury found the union members not guilty. In the end, Darrow's strong attack on mine owners swayed the jury. Their not-guilty verdict caused union leaders throughout the country to rejoice.

At the same time, dams were built on the Snake River to collect water in **reservoirs,** or pools. The water was channeled throughout the Snake River valley to irrigate farmland. Idaho's farmers thrived during World War I (1914–1918), when food shortages caused the price of crops to rise. But farmers suffered when prices fell after the war.

During the Great Depression, a nationwide economic slump of the 1930s, the price of silver also fell, and the demand for lumber came to a halt. Idaho's workers saw their earnings cut in half. To create jobs for some people, the U.S. government oversaw projects to build roads and raise shelters in state parks. In 1938 workers finished the first paved highway between northern and southern Idaho, easing travel through the mountains.

Idaho's economy boomed again during World War II (1939–1945). Miners produced metals needed for weapons, farmers provided food, and factory workers turned out airplane parts, guns, and ammunition. Thousands of men and women trained at air bases in Boise, Pocatello, and Mountain Home.

The Chairman and the Count

During the Great Depression of the 1930s, many people lost their jobs, and poverty was widespread. But some fortunate people still had the time and money to travel. Idaho offered them Sun Valley—the nation's fanciest ski resort.

The resort had been dreamed up by W. Averell Harriman (above left), the chairman of the Union Pacific Railroad. Harriman was trying to figure out a way to attract new passengers. Skiing was becoming popular, so Harriman thought a mountain resort might be the answer.

In 1935 Harriman invited Felix Schaffgotsch, an Austrian count and an expert skier, to the United States. The count agreed to help Harriman choose a place for the resort. Together the two men traveled to the snowcapped peaks of Mount Rainier in Washington. They saw the steep slopes of Yosemite National Park in California, and they visited the dry Wasatch Mountains of Utah. But none of these sites satisfied the count.

Finally, they arrived in Ketchum, Idaho. Nearby was a spectacular valley surrounded by treeless slopes. The snow was deep and powdery—perfect conditions for skiing. There was little wind and plenty of warm sunshine. And at one end of the valley lay the tracks of the Union Pacific Railroad.

The count and Harriman had found Sun Valley (above right). A lodge opened the next year and quickly became a favorite spot for movie stars and other wealthy people. As the resort became more famous, tourists flocked to the area.

During World War II, thousands of sailors trained at Farragut Naval Station in Idaho. The men learned to use snowshoes for assignments in Alaska and Greenland.

After the war, Pend Oreille Lake became a training site for submarine crews and a testing ground for nuclear submarines. In 1949 the U.S. government built a nuclear reactor testing station in Idaho Falls. In 1955 Arco became the first city in the world to get all of its electricity from nuclear power instead of from burning fuels. (Nuclear power is energy that is released from atoms when they are split in a reactor.)

By the 1960s, food-processing plants in southern Idaho were canning and freezing the state's fruits and vegetables. Lumber companies in northern Idaho manufactured plywood, wood pulp, paper containers, and other wood products from the state's timber. In Boise, Pocatello, and Coeur d'Alene, factories made computers and other high-tech goods.

Shipping all of these products to markets became much easier in 1975. That year Idaho gained a seaport when the last of several dams was completed along the Snake and Columbia Rivers. As a result of the dams, oceangoing ships could travel inland as far as Lewiston.

At Lewiston, dockhands load oceangoing ships with grain and other goods.

Skiing is just one of the adventurous activities that tourists can enjoy in Idaho.

Tourism also became a big business. Hikers, hunters, skiers, and other outdoor enthusiasts visited Idaho's wilderness areas. To keep the state beautiful, strict laws prevented road building as well as mining and logging in certain protected areas. And in 1999, Idaho sent one of the first shipments of nuclear waste to the federal Waste Isolation Pilot Project in New Mexico for permanent storage. The shipment marked the beginning of U.S. efforts to safely clean up the nation's nuclear waste.

Although tourism has grown to be the state's third largest industry, some Idahoans believe the state has protected too much land. They argue that mining and logging in wilderness areas would help the state earn more money. Other people disagree. They say that wilderness visitors help the state's economy just as much by spending money for hotels, outdoor equipment, and guides.

While Idahoans clash over the use of wilderness areas, they share a love of their state's natural beauty. By working to solve their differences, Idahoans are planning a better future for their state.

Hot air balloons float over Boise at the Boise River Festival.

In the pioneer town of Idaho City, the state's past comes to life. The city once bustled with gold seekers.

PEOPLE & ECONOMY

Working the Land

For centuries Idaho's rugged landscape kept large numbers of people from settling in the state. But with the discovery of gold in 1860, people braved deserts and mountains to flock to Idaho. Many modern Idahoans can trace their roots to these early miners and to the farmers and loggers who followed.

More than 88 percent of Idaho's 1.3 million residents are white. Their ancestors came from Great Britain, Germany, Ireland, the Netherlands, and the Scandinavian countries. About 8 percent of Idahoans are Latino. Asians and African Americans each number less than 1 percent. Many of their ancestors came to Idaho in the late 1800s to mine or to build railroads.

A large Basque community lives in southwestern Idaho. Their ancestors came from Spain to herd sheep.

Nearly 16,000, or 1.2 percent, of the state's population is Native American. About 3,500 Shoshone and Bannock live on the Fort Hall reservation, and 3,000 Nez Perce live on the Nez Perce reservation. Other Indians reside in cities or on smaller reservations. Many practice their traditional religion, study their native language and history, and play in traditional sporting events. Throughout the year,

Local Native American powwows host dance competitions.

various ceremonies are led to honor salmon, berries, and root plants such as the camas lily.

Nearly half of Idaho's people live in the countryside. About 30 percent have homes in the southwestern part of the state, mostly around Boise—the capital and largest city. Boise and other big towns are located on or near the Snake River. These include Nampa, Twin Falls, Pocatello, Idaho Falls, and Lewiston. Coeur d'Alene is in the Idaho panhandle.

Many buildings from the 1800s still stand in Boise. Visitors can tour Old Fort Boise or the cells of the Old Idaho Penitentiary, a prison that once held stagecoach robbers, horse thieves, and other outlaws.

Idaho has many ghost towns for visitors to explore. Idaho City and Silver City once bustled with miners. Visitors can tour weathered buildings, relax in remodeled saloons, and stroll through cemeteries where many of the miners are buried.

History buffs can hike the Lolo Trail, the path Lewis and Clark followed through central Idaho. Farther south, wheel ruts more than 100 years old trace the path of the Oregon Trail, the old settlers' highway.

At Logger Days in Cascade, Idahoans test their speed at crosscutting timber the old-fashioned way.

Travelers carved their names and initials into Register Rock, a famous landmark along the trail.

Festivals and fairs are held in Idaho throughout the year. The Nez Perce perform traditional dances at the Chief Lookingglass Celebration, a powwow in Kamiah. Each March the nation's top cowboys ride and rope at the Dodge National Circuit Finals Rodeo in Pocatello. At Lumberjack Days in Orofino, loggers demonstrate logrolling.

Idaho has two state fairs—the Eastern Fair at Blackfoot and the Western Fair at Boise. Fairgoers enjoy horse races, food, carnival rides, and music. Farmers exhibit their prize cattle, horses, and sheep.

Idahoans celebrate winter with snow carnivals, ice sculptures, and sled-dog races. Snowmobilers can speed along 5,000 miles of groomed trails. In January, Sun Valley hosts the Duchin Cup Celebrity Ski Race.

A favorite pastime among Idahoans is fishing. In fact, about one out of every three Idahoans has a fishing license. The Henry's Fork of the Snake River is prized as one of the finest trout-fishing streams in the world.

Many Idaho towns host rodeo action.

On the North Fork of the Payette River, rafters maneuver their float through rapids.

Another popular sport is whitewater rafting. With thousands of miles of rapids and other white water, Idaho's rivers tempt daredevils. Outfitters offer guided tours down the Salmon River and other rough waterways.

In the Idaho Panhandle National Forests, a park ranger helps a family spot a bird among the cedar trees.

People from other states come every season of the year to enjoy Idaho's natural beauty. Almost two-thirds of the state is public land—wilderness areas, national forests, and parks. Rugged mountains have given the state one of its nicknames, Gem of the Mountains. Idaho also boasts natural caves, weird rock formations, and ancient lava beds.

Many Idahoans have jobs helping the state's visitors. Hotel clerks, restaurant workers, and rafting and hunting outfitters all have service jobs, which employ nearly 60 percent of Idaho's workforce. The state's bank tellers, doctors, and salespeople are also service workers.

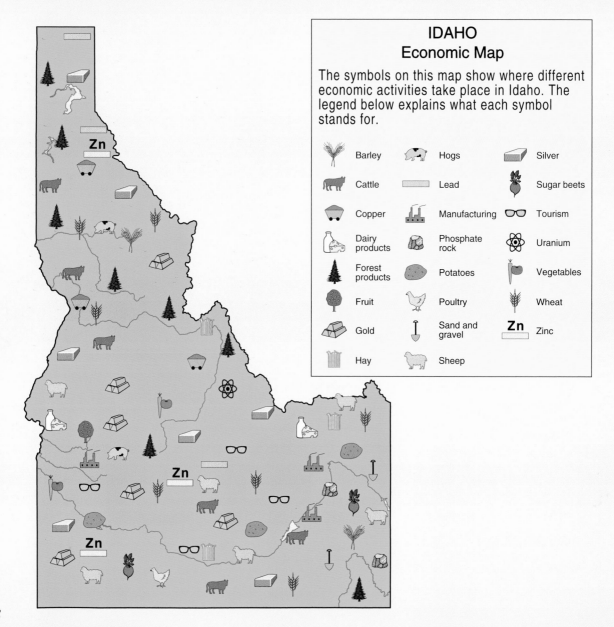

IDAHO
Economic Map

The symbols on this map show where different economic activities take place in Idaho. The legend below explains what each symbol stands for.

Barley		Hogs		Silver	
Cattle		Lead		Sugar beets	
Copper		Manufacturing		Tourism	
Dairy products		Phosphate rock		Uranium	
Forest products		Potatoes		Vegetables	
Fruit		Poultry		Wheat	
Gold		Sand and gravel		Zinc	
Hay		Sheep			

The government employs about 15 percent of Idaho's workforce. Government workers include park rangers, politicians, and other civil servants.

In 1889 the University of Idaho was founded in the town of Moscow. Many students took, and still take, classes in agriculture and farm management. Agriculture still earns the state a lot of money and employs about 7 percent of Idaho's workers.

Idaho leads the nation in producing potatoes, but farmers also grow hay, wheat, barley, and sugar beets. Fruit growers raise apples, cherries, peaches, and pears. Beef cattle and dairy products are also important. Many farmers ship their produce to the Pacific Coast by way of the Snake and Columbia Rivers.

Some of the state's produce goes to food-processing plants within Idaho for packaging. These and other factories in the state employ 12 percent of Idaho's workforce. Around Boise, workers manufacture electrical machinery, computers, and office equipment.

Heaps of potatoes add up to big business in Idaho.

In much of Idaho, logging operations dot the roadsides.

Throughout the state, timber is an important raw material for manufacturers. Lumber companies process raw timber into plywood, particleboard, wood pulp, and paper. Lumber mills also cut logs to the right shape and size for building cabins and houses.

The state's numerous ghost towns remind people that mining was once Idaho's most important industry. But only 1 percent of the workforce has jobs in mines. The area around Coeur d'Alene, known as Silver Valley, has one of the richest silver deposits in the world. Lead, zinc, and copper are also mined in this region.

In the southeast, phosphate rock is mined to make fertilizers. Throughout the state, gemstones such as garnets are found. Whether you call it the Gem State or Gem of the Mountains, Idaho is a jewel in many ways.

THE ENVIRONMENT

Saving the Salmon

 ish have long been important to Idaho's people. For centuries Native Americans depended on abundant stocks of salmon as a main food source. Later, settlers built up a fishing industry that thrived on salmon and trout from Idaho's waters. Sportfishing has since become a big attraction for both residents and tourists.

But by the mid-1900s, the numbers of some species, or types, of fish in Idaho began to drop. Commercial fishing crews were hauling in such huge catches that some species couldn't breed fast enough to keep their populations stable or growing. People were polluting rivers and building dams, making it hard for salmon, trout, sturgeon, and other fish to find food and to produce young.

Icefishing is a popular sport for Idahoans young or old.

51

Pollution comes from many different sources. At mines, minerals are separated from rocks in a process that leaves behind lead and other heavy metals. Over time, these waste metals can seep into waterways. During a rainstorm, the chemicals that farmers use on their fields can wash into streams.

Another source of pollution comes from something natural—soil. Trees and grass hold soil in place. But the soil is disturbed when ranchers graze cattle and when loggers cut timber and build roads to get to trees. Even hikers and other people who

Idaho's rivers are polluted by soil that collects at their bottoms. Grazing sheep cut into hillsides and loosen soil. Then it slides into the rivers.

Roads are a big cause of sediment, which pollutes the nearby rivers.

use land for recreation can loosen soil. Sediment, or dirt, then gradually slides into nearby waterways, making them cloudy.

As the sediment settles to the bottom of a river, it fills spaces between rocks where insects hide. The bugs become trapped, and the fish, who feed on the insects, have trouble finding food. Sediment also can bury the gravel beds at the bottom of a waterway, where fish scoop out nests to spawn, or lay eggs. When sediment fills a nest, it smothers the eggs. Young fish, who hide at the bottom of a stream, get stuck and can't swim out from between the rocks.

Dams create many
obstacles for Idaho's fish.

Dams cause the most danger to river life. These cement walls are built to hold back water, some of which is saved to irrigate crops and lawns during the summer. The rest of the water is released gradually to control the speed of the river's flow. This helps prevent flooding during spring snowmelts.

Many dams have been equipped to produce hydropower, or electricity generated with water-power. As the water passes through the dam, it sets huge turbines, or engines, in motion. The spinning turbines then power generators that produce electricity. Because the generators don't burn fuel, they don't pollute the air.

Dams provide cheap, nonpolluting electricity and irrigation water. But they also harm fish. By slowing the flow of water, dams slow down fish. This is a big problem for young salmon, called smolts. As smolts mature, they move from fresh water to salt water, traveling from their birthplace in Idaho all the way to the Pacific Ocean.

The Department of Fish and Game collects smolts *(left)* to raise and breed in captivity. On the Salmon River, a salmon *(above)* selects a gravel bed for spawning.

Long, difficult journeys for salmon make it easier for bears to catch them.

Before dams, the journey down the Snake and Columbia Rivers took the fish 10 days. Now it lasts a month or more. The extra time gives bears and other predators a much better chance of catching smolts for their next meal. Those who do reach the ocean may arrive too late to be able to adapt to life in salt water.

Dams cause other problems, too. Slow-moving water is warmer than the fish need, so they are more likely to catch diseases. They also get lost more easily without a fast current to direct their journey. Some experts say that 90 percent of all smolts die from turbines, predators, or disease, or simply run out of time to swim to the ocean.

In 1980 the Northwest Power Planning Act formed a council to help the recovery of lost fisheries due to hydropower development. The act helped keep salmon off of the federal Endangered Species Act (ESA) in the early 1980s.

But the salmon continued to decline. In 1991 and 1992, Snake River salmon were listed for ESA protection. And in 1994, people petitioned for ESA protection for the Snake River wild steelhead trout.

To help save salmon, some Idahoans want to increase the flow of water through dams during the spring, when most smolts swim to the ocean. Others want to decrease the water in reservoirs to make it flow like a natural river and shorten travel time for smolts. Engineers have built bypasses at the dams to catch smolts, which are then put in barges and taken to the ocean.

Some Idahoans are working on other projects to improve conditions for the state's fish. Some programs teach people to leave the area along streams alone, so sediment doesn't get into the water.

To limit the flow of chemicals into rivers, farmers are learning to be more careful about how they apply chemicals to their fields. After a mining job is complete, laws require mining companies to clean up. Rules also set limits on the size and number of certain species fishers can catch and forbid fishing during spawning periods. And in 2000, salmon supporters asked the government to destroy dams in

It is important for the survival of the salmon that the Snake River be kept clean.

the lower Snake River so that the area could return to its natural state.

With these efforts, Idaho species such as chinook and sockeye salmon, steelhead trout, bull trout, cut-throat trout, and white sturgeon may be saved from extinction. Through careful planning, Idahoans will be able to preserve the state's fish populations for the future.

Sockeye salmon were listed as endangered in 1991. Since then Idahoans have done much to ensure their survival.

Fun Facts

The world's largest potato chip is at the Potato Museum in Blackfoot, Idaho. The chip measures 14 inches by 25 inches.

One of the largest diamonds ever found in the United States, nearly 20 carats, was uncovered near McCall, Idaho.

In 1974 daredevil Evil Knievel tried to leap across the Snake River canyon in Idaho on his rocket-powered motorcycle. He didn't make it because his safety parachute opened too soon. Knievel floated to the ground and was not seriously injured.

The world's first chairlift for skiers began operating in 1936 at the Sun Valley resort in Idaho. Engineer Jim Curran based his design on the device he had invented to load bananas onto ships — but instead of hooks, he used chairs.

Balanced Rock near Buhl, Idaho, stands 40 feet high on a base that's only a few feet thick.

At Hagerman Fossil Beds in southern Idaho are fossils of ancient horses and other animals that lived between two and three million years ago.

On August 13, 1896, outlaw Butch Cassidy robbed the Bank of Montpelier in Idaho of more than $7,000. A replay of the shoot-out is held every summer on Montpelier's Main Street.

Balanced Rock

STATE SONG

Idaho's state song was written in 1915 by a student at the University of Idaho. Known then as "Our Idaho," it became a popular school song. Later, in 1931, Idaho state lawmakers adopted the song, with a new name, as the official state song.

HERE WE HAVE IDAHO

Words by McKinley Helm and Albert J. Tompkins
Music by Sallie Hume Douglas

You can hear "Here We Have Idaho" by visiting this website:
<http://www2.state.id.us/gov/fyi/symbols/index.htm>

AN IDAHO RECIPE

Idaho's climate provides nearly perfect growing conditions for potatoes. Try spicing up your spuds with this fiery recipe.

POTATO NACHOS

1 large Idaho potato
2 tablespoons canned green chilies, drained
¼ teaspoon salt
¾ cup taco sauce or salsa

¾ cup (3 ounces) shredded cheddar cheese
½ cup chopped green onions

1. Clean potato with warm water. Have an adult help you cut potato into thin slices, about ½ inch thick.
2. Put slices in a microwave-safe pie plate or shallow baking dish. Sprinkle potato slices with salt, and brush half of the taco sauce on them.
3. Cover plate with microwave-safe plastic wrap. Microwave slices on high 4–5 minutes, until potatoes are tender. Rotate plate a half turn after 2 minutes.
4. Brush potato slices with remaining taco sauce. Add green chilies, green onions, and cheese.
5. Cover and microwave on high until cheese melts. Enjoy!

HISTORICAL TIMELINE

11,000 B.C. Native Americans move into the area that later became Idaho.

A.D. 1750 Nez Perce and Shoshone Indians acquire horses.

1805 Lewis and Clark reach the Idaho area.

1834 Fort Hall is built on the Snake River.

1842 Father Pierre-Jean de Smet builds the Cataldo Mission.

1846 The United States takes control of Oregon Country.

1848 The Oregon Country is renamed the Oregon Territory.

1855 U.S. government and Nez Perce leaders sign a treaty in which the Nez Perce agree to give up much of their homeland.

1860 Gold is discovered at Orofino Creek.

1863 The Idaho Territory is created.

1878 The U.S. government defeats the Bannock Indians in the Bannock War.

1884 Silver is discovered in Idaho's panhandle.

1890 Idaho becomes the 43rd state.

1899 Bunker Hill mine is blown up.

1905 Idaho's first dam is completed on the Snake River.

1936 Sun Valley resort opens.

1938 Northern and southern Idaho are linked by a paved highway.

1955 Arco becomes the first town in the world to have all of its electricity generated by nuclear power.

1975 The Columbia-Snake River Inland Waterway is completed, making Lewiston an inland seaport.

1990 Idaho celebrates 100 years of statehood.

1999 Idaho sends a shipment of nuclear waste to a new permanent storage facility in New Mexico.

2001 The Snowshoe fire burns over 23,000 acres of Idaho wilderness and threatens the town of Landmark.

OUTSTANDING IDAHOANS

C. K. Ah-Fong

William E. Borah

Carol Ryrie Brink

C. K. Ah-Fong (1845–1927) became a pioneer when he left his native China in the 1860s and settled near Boise. He set up a medical practice and drug shop. Filling a need for qualified doctors, Ah-Fong gained respect from his patients—white as well as Asian.

William E. Borah (1865–1940) was a politician from Illinois. He moved to Boise in 1891 and began practicing law. First elected to the U.S. Senate in 1907, Borah held the position until his death. Though he was Republican, Borah sided with neither political party. Nicknamed the Great Opposer, he often voted against the ideas of his Republican Party colleagues.

Gutzon Borglum (1867–1941), a sculptor born near Bear Lake, Idaho, directed a team of workers as they blasted and chiseled Mount Rushmore National Memorial in South Dakota. Begun in 1927, the 60-foot carving features the faces of four U.S. presidents and took 14 years to complete.

Carol Ryrie Brink (1895–1981), born in Moscow, Idaho, was an author who wrote mostly for young people. In 1936 she won the Newbery Medal for *Caddie Woodlawn*, a book based on her grandmother's pioneer life. Altogether, Brink wrote more than two dozen books.

Frank Church (1924–1984), born in Boise, was a U.S. senator from Idaho for 24 years, from 1956 to 1980. Church chaired the powerful Senate Committee on Foreign Relations and the Select Committee on Intelligence. He also worked to preserve Idaho's wilderness.

Frank Church

Mourning Dove (1884–1936) was a writer born near Bonner's Ferry, Idaho. Part Okanogan and part Colville Indian, she wrote about the lives and folklore of Native Americans in *Coyote Stories* and in *Cogewea, the Half Blood.*

Joseph R. Garry

Joseph R. Garry (1910–1975), a Coeur d'Alene Indian from Plummer, Idaho, served two terms as a state senator in the 1950s and 1960s. From 1953 to 1959, Garry also was president of the National Congress of American Indians, an organization working for the rights of Native Americans.

Emma Edwards Green (1856–1942) was an artist who taught painting classes in Boise. In 1891 she was asked to enter a competition to design the Idaho state seal. Green's artwork won, making her the first woman to design an official state seal. Her design was revised in 1957, but Green's original is designated an Official Copy.

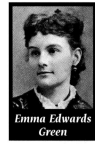

Emma Edwards Green

Mariel Hemingway (born 1961), from Mill Valley, Idaho, is an actress who has starred in several movies, including *Manhattan, Personal Best,* and *Deconstructing Harry.* She is the granddaughter of the famous writer Ernest Hemingway.

Mariel Hemingway

Walter Johnson (1887–1946), one of the greatest pitchers in baseball history, was known for throwing a ball so fast it seemed invisible. Johnson's entire 21-year career was with the Washington Senators. He was among the first five players to be elected to the Baseball Hall of Fame. Johnson grew up in Weiser, Idaho.

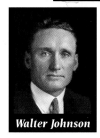

Walter Johnson

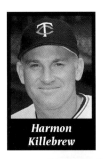

Harmon Killebrew

Edwin R. Peterson

Gracie Pfost

Ezra Pound

Harmon Killebrew (born 1936), a baseball player from Payette, Idaho, led or tied the American League in home runs six times and in runs batted in three times. After retiring from the Minnesota Twins in 1975, Killebrew became a sportscaster. He was elected to the National Baseball Hall of Fame in 1984.

Morlan Nelson (born 1916) is an activist who started the Snake River Birds of Prey Natural Area to protect land uniquely suited for peregrine falcons, eagles, and other endangered birds of prey. Nelson has been an active leader at the World Center for Birds of Prey in Boise, where he has lived since 1948.

Edwin R. Peterson (1921–1999), a businessman, invented the backup beeper, which warns people to stay clear of backing vehicles. Peterson made the first Bac-A-Larm in his basement in Boise. In 1947 he founded PRECO, Inc., a company that later manufactured and distributed the alarm and other electronic products.

Gracie Pfost (1906–1965) was a politician who championed the federal construction of a high, multi-purpose dam at Hells Canyon. In 1952 Pfost became the first female Idahoan elected to the U.S. House of Representatives. She grew up on a farm near Boise.

Ezra Pound (1885–1972) was a poet born in Hailey, Idaho. Pound, who experimented with different forms of verse, was a major influence on modern literature. Pound's work includes *The Cantos* and *The Pisan Cantos*.

Sacagawea (1786?–1812), a Shoshone Indian, was born in what later became eastern Idaho. She helped guide the Lewis and Clark expedition to the Pacific Ocean and served as an interpreter and peacekeeper along the way.

Jack R. Simplot (born 1909) started the J. R. Simplot Company, a potato-processing empire, at the age of 14. Known as Idaho's Potato King, Simplot created instant potatoes and frozen French fries. Raised in a one-room cabin in Delco, Idaho, Simplot became one of the richest men in Idaho.

Jack R. Simplot

Marion Barton Skaggs (1888–1976), from American Falls, Idaho, bought his father's grocery store in 1915. By 1926 Skaggs was running a chain of more than 400 stores, and the company merged with Safeway grocery stores. Skagg's leadership helped make Safeway one of the largest food chains in the world.

Picabo Street (born 1971) is from Sun Valley, Idaho. In the 1994 Olympics she won a silver medal, and in 1995 and 1996 she won the World Cup title. In 1998 Street overcame a serious knee injury to win the Olympic gold for downhill skiing.

Picabo Street

Jackson Sundown (1863–1923) was a Nez Perce horseman from central Idaho. At the age of 53, competing against men half his age, he became the first Native American to win the World Saddle Bronco Championship at the 1916 Pendleton Round-Up.

Jackson Sundown

Lana Turner (1920–1995), from Wallace, Idaho, became an actress when she was discovered by moviemakers while drinking a soda in a Hollywood diner. Among her best-known films are *The Postman Always Rings Twice* and *Peyton Place*.

Kitty Wilkins (1857?–1936), a horse dealer, started her business at the age of 22 with just one horse. Working out of her family's ranch in Bruneau, Idaho, Wilkins became so successful at selling the animals that by the 1890s she had earned a national reputation as Idaho's Horse Queen.

Lana Turner

FACTS-AT-A-GLANCE

Nickname: Gem State

Song: "Here We Have Idaho"

Motto: *Esto Perpetua* (Let it be perpetual)

Flower: syringa

Tree: western white pine

Bird: mountain bluebird

Gemstone: star garnet

Insect: monarch butterfly

Fish: cutthroat trout

Date and ranking of statehood: July 3, 1890, the 43rd state

Capital: Boise

Area: 82,751 square miles

Rank in area, nationwide: 13

Average January temperature: 23°F

Average July temperature: 67°F

Idaho's state flag shows the state seal, which has symbols of mining and agriculture. The woman stands for justice, liberty, and equality.

POPULATION GROWTH

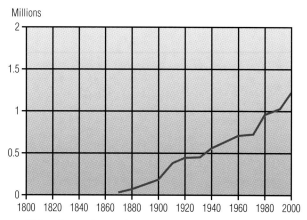

Millions

This chart shows how Idaho's population has grown from 1870 to 2000.

Idaho's state seal was adopted in 1891. The seal shows a woman holding scales and a spear, representing justice, liberty, and equality. The miner, elk head, pine tree, and grain represent the state's natural resources.

Population: 1,293,953 (2000 census)

Rank in population, nationwide: 39th

Major cities and populations: (2000 census) Boise (185,787), Nampa (51,867), Pocatello (51,466), Idaho Falls (50,730), Meridian (34,919)

U.S. senators: 2

U.S. representatives: 2

Electoral votes: 4

Natural resources: cobalt, copper, garnet, gold, lead, limestone, molybdenum, phosphate, rock, sand and gravel, silver, timber, uranium, water, zinc

Agricultural products: beef cattle, cherries, hay, milk, peaches, potatoes, sugar beets, wheat

Mining: cobalt, copper, garnet, gold, lead, phosphate, rock, silver, uranium, zinc

Manufactured goods: computers, electrical equipment, farm equipment, fertilizer, food products, lumber, paper products, particleboard

WHERE IDAHOANS WORK

Services—58 percent (services include jobs
in trade; community, social, and
personal services; finance, insurance,
and real estate; transportation,
communication, and utilities)

Government—15 percent

Manufacturing—12 percent

Agriculture—7 percent

Construction—7 percent

Mining—1 percent

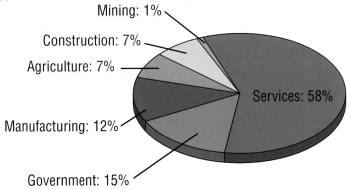

GROSS STATE PRODUCT

Services—55 percent (services include
community, social, & personal services;
finance, insurance, & real estate; transportation, communication, & utilities)

Manufacturing—19 percent

Government—13 percent

Agriculture—6 percent

Construction—6 percent

Mining—1 percent

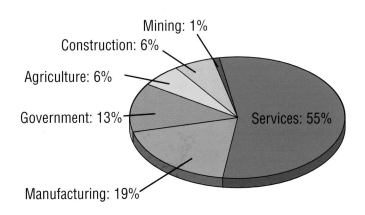

IDAHO WILDLIFE

Mammals: bighorn sheep, black bear, bobcat, chipmunk, cougar, coyote, deer, elk, gray wolf, grizzly bear, mink, moose, pronghorn, Rocky Mountain sheep

Birds: American white pelican, bald eagle, Chukar partridge, golden eagle, hawk, Pacific loon, peregrine falcon, pheasant, snowy egret, whooping crane

Amphibians and reptiles: bullfrog, desert horned lizard, loggerhead sea turtle, western racer, western rattlesnake, western toad

Fish: Bonneville cutthroat trout, burbot, chinook salmon, kamloops trout, sockeye salmon, steelhead trout, sturgeon

Trees: birch, cottonwood, Douglas fir, Engelmann spruce, hemlock, pine, quaking aspen, red cedar, western larch, white fir

Wild plants: black-eyed Susan, buttercup, heliotrope, Idaho bluebells, Macfarlane's four-o'clock, Nuttall's sunflower, primrose

Bald Eagle

PLACES TO VISIT

Bruneau Dunes State Park, Bruneau
See the tallest sand dunes in North America. The park features fishing, camping, and Idaho's only public observatory.

City of Rocks National Reserve, Alamo
Granite columns loom high above this 500-acre valley. An important landmark for pioneers on the California Trail, visitors can still see where travelers wrote their names on the rocks.

Craters of the Moon National Monument, Arco
This 83-square-mile national monument boasts an array of volcanic features, such as cinder cones, lava tubes, and more.

Hells Canyon National Recreation Area, near Lewiston
At 7,900 feet, Hells Canyon is the deepest river gorge in North America. Nez Perce pictographs can be found in caves and on the canyon's walls.

Idaho Museum of Natural History, Pocatello
Learn about the state's natural history through exhibits and interactive displays. Kids can check out the Discovery Room and the Odyssey Portal.

Nez Perce National Historical Park, Spalding
This branch of the park features sites designated to honor the history and legends of the Nez Perce people.

Shoshone Falls, Snake River
Visit the Niagara of the West, where white water plunges more than 212 feet, bathing the area in a rainbow of mist.

Silver City Historical Area, Silver City
Established in 1864, Silver City has maintained nearly 75 of its original structures. Visit the antique-filled Idaho Hotel and the Post Office-Drugstore.

Silver Valley Historical Area, near Kellogg
Visitors learn about the valley's rich mining history and can take a walking tour of the area's ghost towns or pan for gold like the early miners.

Snake River Birds of Prey Natural Area, Boise
See hawks, eagles, falcons, and other birds of prey on this 80-mile stretch along the Snake River.

Hells Canyon

ANNUAL EVENTS

Winter Carnival, McCall—*January–February*

Lionel Hampton Jazz Festival, Moscow—*February*

Dodge National Circuit Finals Rodeo, Pocatello—*March*

Dogwood Festival of the Lewis-Clark Valley, Lewiston—*April*

Payette Apple Blossom Festival—*May*

Western Days, Twin Falls—*June*

Gem County Cherry Festival, Emmett—*June*

Teton Valley Hot Air Balloon Festival & Mountain Arts Fair, Driggs—*July*

Paul Bunyan Days, Saint Maries—*August–September*

Trailing of the Sheep Festival, Ketchum—*October*

Coeur d'Alene Fantasy in Lights—*November–January*

LEARN MORE ABOUT IDAHO

BOOKS

General

Fradin, Dennis Brindell. *Idaho*. Chicago: Children's Press, 1998. For older readers.

George, Charles, and Linda George. *Idaho*. New York: Children's Press, 2000.

Special Interest

Bowen, Andy Russell. *The Back of Beyond*. Minneapolis: Carolrhoda Books, Inc., 1997. Experience the story of the expedition of Meriwether Lewis and William Clark as they explore the land that would later become the western United States.

Dippold, Joel. *Picabo Street: Downhill Dynamo*. Minneapolis: Lerner Publications Company, 1998. This biography covers the life of the young skier who won a silver medal in the 1994 Winter Olympics and a gold medal at the 1998 Olympics.

Rifkin, Mark. *The Nez Perce Indians*. New York: Chelsea House, 1993. Learn more about the history and culture of Idaho's largest and most powerful Native American group.

Rowland, Della. *The Story of Sacajawea: Guide to Lewis and Clark*. New York: Dell Publishing, 1999. Read about the life of the woman who helped guide Lewis and Clark through the uncharted terrain of the western United States.

Fiction

Bartholomew, Sandra. *Sara of Sun Valley: An Idaho Adventure.* Windsor, CT: Story House Dolls, 1999. Sara dreams of skiing in the Olympics, but an accident forces her and her family to rethink their priorities.

Duey, Kathleen. *Celou Sudden Shout; Idaho, 1827.* New York: Aladdin Paperbacks, 1998. Celou Sudden Shout, a Shoshone girl, struggles to free her mother and brothers from an enemy tribe.

Hamilton, Morse. *The Garden of Eden Motel.* New York: Greenwillow, 1999. Set in the 1950s, 11-year-old Dal travels to rural Idaho with his new stepfather. Instead of Wild West excitement, he finds courage and friendship in a small, sleepy town. For older readers.

Murphy, Jim. *West to a Land of Plenty: The Diary of Teresa Angelino Viscardi, New York to Idaho Territory, 1883.* New York: Scholastic, 1998. This fictional diary tells the story of Teresa Viscardi as she and her family move from her beloved New York to Idaho Territory.

WEBSITES

Access Idaho
<http://www.state.id.us/>
The state's official website includes information about living and working in Idaho, a history link, and a kid's page.

Idaho Travel and Tourism Guide
<http://www.visitid.org/>
Learn more about Idaho through this website—everything from the state's natural attractions to its historical sites and festivals.

The Idaho Statesman
<http://www.idahostatesman.com/news/daily/default.shtml>
The *Idaho Statesman* is Boise's largest daily newspaper. The paper covers local and national news, as well as the area's cultural events.

Idaho, A Portrait
<http://www.pbs.org/idahoportrait/>
Explore the geology, history, and people of Idaho through PBS's interactive tour of the state.

PRONUNCIATION GUIDE

Bannock (BAN-uhk)

Boise (BOY-see)

Borah (BOHR-uh)

Coeur d'Alene (KOHR duh-LAYN)

Kalispel (KAL-uh-spehl)

Kutenai (KOOT-ihn-ay)

Lewiston (LOO-uhs-tuhn)

Nampa (NAM-puh)

Nez Perce (NEHZ PURS)

Orofino (awr-uh-FEE-noh)

Paiute (PY-yoot)

Pend Oreille (pahn duh-RAY)

Pocatello (poh-kuh-TEHL-oh)

Shoshone (shuh-SHOHN)

Skiers enjoy the slopes at Sun Valley
Ski Resort in Idaho

GLOSSARY

constitution: the system of basic laws or rules of government, society, or organization; the document in which these laws or rules are written

glacier: a large body of ice and snow that moves slowly over land

irrigation: a method of watering land by directing water through canals, pipes, ditches, or sprinklers

labor union: an organization responsible for improving and protecting the wages, benefits, and general working conditions of workers who pay membership dues

missionary: a person sent out by a religious group to spread its beliefs to other people

plateau: a large, relatively flat area that stands above the surrounding land

reservation: public land set aside by the government to be used by Native Americans

reservoir: a place where water is collected and stored for later use

treaty: an agreement between two or more groups, usually having to do with peace or trade

INDEX

PHOTO ACKNOWLEDGMENTS

Cover photographs by © Raymond Gehman/CORBIS (left) and © Jacqui Hurst/CORBIS (right); PresentationMaps.com, pp. 1, 8, 9, 48; © Michael T. Sedam/CORBIS, pp. 2–3; © Jim Zuckerman/CORBIS, p. 3; © Patrick Johns/CORBIS, pp. 4, 7, 16, 41, 51; © Jan Butchofsky-Houser/CORBIS, p. 6; © Buddy Mays/TRAVEL STOCK, pp. 10, 17 (right), 41, 46, 51, 55 (right), 75; Kenneth C. Poertner, pp. 11, 45, 49, 80; © Patrick Cone, p. 12; Veda Scherer/Laatsch-Hupp Photo, p. 13; © Jerry Hennen, p. 14; © David Dvorak Jr., p. 15 (left); Idaho Department of Parks & Recreation, p. 15 (right); Norma Watts, pp. 17 (left), 53; Idaho State Historical Society, pp. 19 (659), 23 (991), 28 (78-208.135), 30 inset (2377), 31 right (3796), 35 right (79-124.32), 36 (D60.171.0004), 66 top (81-2.32), 66 second from top (2252), 67 top (80-151), 67 second from top (71-72.1), 68 second from bottom (82-2.53), 69 top (77-2.45); Denver Public Library, Western History Coll., pp. 20, 30; Haynes Foundation Collection, Montana Historical Society, Helena, MT pp. 21, 31 (left); Pacific University Archives, Forest Grove, OR, p. 22; © James L. Amos/CORBIS, p. 24; Oregon Historical Society #485, p. 26; Smithsonian Institution, Nat'l Anthropological Archives, p. 27; © Bettmann/CORBIS, pp. 33 (left), 33 (right); Sun Valley News Bureau/Historic Photo Coll., Univ. of ID-Moscow, p. 35 (left); Jim Soyk Jr./Port of Lewiston, p. 37; © Karl Weatherly/CORBIS, p. 38; © Dave G. Houser/CORBIS, p. 39; Bill Billingham/F-Stock, Inc., p. 40; Jim Nau, p. 42; Donna Cutbirth, p. 44; Jim Hughes/Idaho Panhandle National Forests, p. 47, 50; Margaret Crader, p.52; Idaho Deptartment of Fish & Game, p. 54 (D. Ronayne), 55 (left, D. Ronayne); © Paul A. Souders/CORBIS, p. 56; © Wolfgang Kaehler/-CORBIS, p. 58; © Natalie Fobes/CORBIS, p. 59; Jack Lindstrom, p. 60; © Morton Beebe, S. F./CORBIS, p. 61; Tim Seeley, pp. 63, 71 (top), 72 (both); Latah County Historical Society, p. 66 (second from bottom); Boise State University Library, Frank Church Coll., p. 66 (bottom); Hollywood Book & Poster, p. 67 (second from bottom), 69 (bottom); © Underwood & Underwood/CORBIS, p. 67 (bottom); MN Twins, p. 68 (top); Burns Studio, p. 68 (second from top); © David Lees/CORBIS, p. 68 (bottom); © Wally McNamee/CORBIS, p. 69 (second from top); National Park Service, Nez Perce Nat'l Historic Park Coll., p. 69 (second from bottom); Jean Matheny, p. 70 (top); © Buddy Mays/CORBIS, p. 73;